film posters of the 60s
the essential movies of the decade

from the reel poster gallery collection
edited by tony nourmand and graham marsh

aurum press

First published in 1997 by
Aurum Press Limited
25 Bedford Avenue
London WC1B 3AT

2005 2004 2003
10   9   8   7

A catalogue record for this book is available
from the British Library.

ISBN 1 85410 513 2

Art direction and design by Graham Marsh
Page make-up by Trevor Gray

Printed in Singapore by C.S. Graphics

ACKNOWLEDGEMENTS

SPECIAL THANKS TO:
Richard Allen
Joe Burtis
Glyn Callingham
Tony Crawley
The Crew from the Island
Roxanna Hajiani
John Kisch
Bruce Marchant
June Marsh
Thomas Milne
Hamid Joseph Nourmand
Gabrielle Pantucci
Ken Schacter
Philip Shalam
Yasumasa Takahashi
X-Man

The Reel Poster Gallery
72 Westbourne Grove
London W2 5SH
Tel: +44 (0)20 7727 4488
Fax: +44 (0)20 7727 4499

Web Site: www.reelposter.com
Email: info@reelposter.com

contents

reelin' in the years

Invented by the Lumière brothers in 1885, the cinema has established trends and set people dreaming from the silent era to the present day. Although directors like Griffith, Eisenstein, Lang, Ford and Hitchcock were largely ignored by intellectuals of their day, their films are now at the heart of our culture. In fact, the cinema seems to have shaped the twentieth century more than any other art form.

Originally designed to attract attention and create desire, film posters were the principal way of telling people what was showing at their local cinema. Today, the imagery of the film poster has come to be known as 'key art'. It is expected to unlock, in perhaps sixty seconds or less, the heart of the film, while at the same time generating enough interest to open the public's wallet.

Posters would accompany the films they were designed to promote from one cinema to the next. Those that survived were returned to the distributors when the film's run had ended. With studios turning out an average of one film a week and always being cost-conscious, archiving this material was never a priority. In fact, when studio storerooms were full, film posters, having served their purpose, were usually destroyed. In other cases, extensive usage, wars, fires and all kinds of natural disasters have helped to make the vintage film poster scarce.

Today, as artefacts of an earlier period, movie posters are viewed in a different light. They are being collected by more and more people. For film buffs, they bring back nostalgic movie-going memories. The unique effect that comes from merging illustrations, lettering, layout and colour to create a 'movie-at-a-glance' image interests graphic designers. Historians and social scientists know that the study of films and their posters can provide significant insight into how our lifestyles and values have changed over time. The constant flux of fashions, prejudices, propaganda and social customs from distinctive and changing eras can all be found in film poster art. Encompassing, as it does, a vast range of styles and designs, the film poster appeals to an endless array of tastes.

Poster collecting is based on an almost naïve attraction to a combination of nostalgia, personal association, film and design appeal. In 1979, I purchased my first original film poster – an American poster

Dr. Strangelove Or: How I Learned To Stop Worrying And Love The Bomb (1964)
US 41 × 27 in. (104 × 69 cm)
Art by Tomi Ungerer

Peter Sellers · George C. Scott

In Stanley Kubrick's

Dr. Strangelove

Or:
How
I Learned
To
Stop
Worrying
And
Love
The
Bomb

the hot-line suspense comedy

also starring **Sterling Hayden** · **Keenan Wynn** · **Slim Pickens** and introducing **Tracy Reed** (as "Miss Foreign Affairs")

Screenplay by **Stanley Kubrick, Peter George & Terry Southern**   Based on the book "Red Alert" by Peter George

Produced & Directed by **Stanley Kubrick** · A Columbia Pictures Release for *Apocalypse Now*. I was instantly hooked. I occasionally picked up duplicates and exchanged them with other collectors for material I really wanted. Over the past eighteen years, I have never stopped looking for posters. By 1992, my collecting habit had become a full-time job. My collector friend, Bruce Marchant, and I became completely absorbed by an exciting and adventurous paper chase. Our hunt took us around Europe and America and brought us face to face with horror stories of people casually overlooking film posters, most notably, a butcher in Oregon (also the owner of the local cinema) who was systematically working his way through posters from the turn of the century to wrap his meat. Needless to say, the one rare occasion where we do stumble upon a real gem makes the entire journey worthwhile and enables us to look back and laugh. With our pure delight in the film poster as an art form, we eventually conceived the idea of making them available to the gaze of those who have not yet experienced their enchantment. The Reel Poster Gallery, opened in 1995, was the result.

I met Graham Marsh last year through our mutual friend Glyn Callingham. I had seen and admired their book, *The Cover Art of Blue Note Records*. Graham expressed an interest in doing a series of books on film posters by the decade, focusing mainly on their design. The idea appealed to me since each volume would enable us to show posters of all film genres and types of design representing each individual decade. I believe that a 'good' poster not only portrays the film for which it was designed, but that ultimately its image perfectly represents the era in which it was born.

As was formerly the case with filmmakers, film posters and their designers never received the recognition which they deserved. Today, as well as being collectables, film posters are increasingly considered works of art and important historic documents.

Film posters of the 60s is the first in the series. By no means the ultimate selection, what follows is simply a small collection which we hope you will enjoy.

TONY NOURMAND

**Once Upon A Time In The West /
C'Era Una Volta II West** (1969)
Italian 79 × 55 in. (201 × 140 cm)

C'ERA UNA VOLTA IL WEST con HENRY FONDA CLAUDIA CARDINALE JASON ROBARDS
nel ruolo di armonica
REGIA DI SERGIO LEONE GABRIELE FERZETTI CHARLES BRONSON PAOLO STOPPA
E IN ORDINE ALFABETICO
TECHNICOLOR® TECHNISCOPE® JACK ELAM LIONEL STANDER WOODY STRODE FRANK WOLFF KEENAN WYNN

hollywood hipsters, celluloid style ...

In *Breakfast At Tiffany's* Audrey Hepburn's appearance as Holly Golightly brought a whole new meaning to pared down glamour. From the Givenchy-designed wardrobe of snappy little dresses to the huge lollipop shaped sunglasses, high-rise hair and kittenish attitude – a look just as desirable today as it was in 1961.

Movies have always had a habit of elevating everyday objects and clothes to cult status. On the big screen even the smallest details become as glamorous and cool as the stars that wear them.

Steve McQueen set the standard for cool as the anti-hero cop in *Bullitt*. Wearing a navy blue cashmere turtleneck sweater and driving a drab green 1967 390 GT fastback Mustang, he was the hippest police Lieutenant ever to hit the streets of San Francisco. It was a lethal combination. The out-of-town gunsels, in their black Dodge Charger, stood no chance when they went head to head with McQueen in the now-classic car chase. The streets of San Francisco were again safe until Lee Marvin, left for dead on Alcatraz, came back to demand his wedge of cash from the Organization in *Point Blank*. Their problem was Marvin did not accept credit cards ... the town was once again steaming.

In 1962 Sean Connery as James Bond toppled two of America's biggest female icons, the young and beautiful Elizabeth Taylor and Doris Day, the eternal screen virgin. He became the biggest international star of the decade. Without a doubt Connery is entitled to the lion's share of credit for the success of James Bond. Turnbull and Asser, the famous men's clothiers on Jermyn Street, is where *Dr No* director Terence Young took Connery for his initial wardrobe. There

he was transformed by tailor Anthony Sinclair, from a Scots body-builder into the epitome of an English gentleman – albeit one with a licence to kill. Throw-away one-liners, assorted gadgets and drop-dead gorgeous women were standard issue in Bond films. But it was a silver Aston Martin DB-5 with modifications that was transported into the realms of mythology when driven by our cool hero in *Goldfinger*. In the early Bond films the combination of material and mechanical tailoring was impeccable, indeed invincible – nobody got the drop on 007.

At the other end of the spy movie spectrum, Michael Caine alias Harry Palmer grooved around London looking for *The Ipcress File*. With his unemotional dead-pan delivery, shorty raincoat and black framed glasses he must have been looking the other way as he passed James Bond's tailor. Not many people know this, but composer John Barry who wrote the Bond theme also scored the eerie music for *The Ipcress File*.

The 60s version of the 1930s according to Hollywood belonged to *Bonnie and Clyde*: they were fashion plates with a ba'ad attitude. No self-respecting fashion victim was safe from the duo's influence. The streets of every metropolis were filled to capacity with slinkily dressed, beret-wearing girls on the arms of men in pinstriped, wide-lapelled suits.

Barbarella did her thing in sexy space suits while Anthony Perkins' alter ego Norman Bates was taking care of business at the Bates Motel. In Hitchcock's *Psycho* he wore a corduroy Ivy League suit as sharp as his mother's knife. Meanwhile, across town Dustin

French 'New Wave' meets American Film Noir in **Le Samouraï**. (Detail from poster on page 73.)

Hoffman as *The Graduate* scored with Mrs Robinson sporting a seersucker jacket and button-down shirt – true Ivy Leaguers were rightly confused.

The decade surfaced some memorable romantic movies and one of the coolest was *Un Homme Et Une Femme (A Man And A Woman)*. Jean-Louis Trintigant and Anouk Aimee walking on the beach at Deauville in their stylish sheepskin coats and then climbing into, successively, Trintigant's red Mustang and a hotel bed – all to the accompaniment of a lush soundtrack by Francis Lai. The sales of teach yourself French books and sheepskin coats went through the roof.

The culture shock was seismic when *My Fair Lady* opened in the same year as The Beatles film *A Hard Day's Night*... . Musicals were in: none more elegant than *The Umbrellas of Cherbourg*. Ice queen Catherine Deneuve kept warm in a knee-length trenchcoat of which Thomas Burberry would have been proud. And he would certainly approved of Alain Delon's trenchcoat-wearing, existentialist hit-man Jef Costello, who had a passion for stealing Citroën DS's in Jean-Pierre Melville's classic masterpiece *Le Samouraï*.

Blow-Up, Antonioni's quintessential 'Swinging Sixties' movie had everything on the menu. Pop culture to go, complete with a side-order of great music from The Yardbirds a score by Herbie Hancock and clothes rails full of fab gear. Things happen to David Hemmings as a photographer caught in a passive life-style. He rubs shoulders with Vanessa Redgrave, snaps Verushka and cavorts with doe-eyed, white-lipsticked dolly birds. He even gets to watch a tennis match without a ball in sight. Like understatement.

Everyone smoked in 60s movies, from Eastwood's trademark cheroots to James Bond's Balkan and Turkish mixture cigarettes made for him by Morlands of Grosvenor Street. The black tobacco of Gitanes and Gauloises were the preferred smoke of the French 'New Wave' congregation while large cigars were de rigueur for the 'Mr. Bigs', high rollers and saloon keepers, and James Coburn without his Zippo lighter in *In Like Flint* would be like Miles Davis without his trumpet.

'What we've got here is a failure to communicate', a sentiment that did not apply sartorially to Paul Newman, who, as *Cool Hand Luke* was doing time in the hippest set of prison duds you've ever seen on a chain-gang. Unlike once upon a time in the west when even the humble poncho on the back of a squinting Clint Eastwood looked menacing. However some western movie experts are still convinced that director Sergio Leone supplied a bullet-proof poncho to Eastwood in *A Fistful of Dollars*.

Ironically, fashion from the 60s, in some form or other is back in vogue, and there is renewed interest in classic cars of the period. Even Minis, the true stars of *The Italian Job* have been updated for today's market, while original film posters that can still restore fading sixties memories to all those who tuned in, turned on, and dropped out are being elevated to cult status by a new generation of movie buffs. Like a wise old sage once said, 'What goes around, comes around'.

GRAHAM MARSH

**Les Parapluies De Cherbourg
(The Umbrellas Of Cherbourg)** (1964)
Japanese 60 × 20 in. (152 × 51 cm)

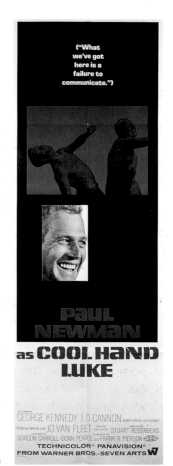

Cool Hand Luke (1967)
US 60 × 20 in. (152 × 51 cm)

The Graduate (1967)
US 41 × 27 in. (104 × 69 cm)
(Style B)

The Graduate (1967)
US 41 × 27 in. (104 × 69 cm)
(Style A)

JOSEPH E. LEVINE
PRESENTS
A
MIKE NICHOLS
LAWRENCE TURMAN
PRODUCTION

THE GRADUATE

STARRING
ANNE BANCROFT AND **DUSTIN HOFFMAN** · **KATHARINE ROSS**
SCREENPLAY BY   SONGS BY
CALDER WILLINGHAM AND **BUCK HENRY** **PAUL SIMON**
PERFORMED BY   PRODUCED BY
SIMON AND **GARFUNKEL** **LAWRENCE TURMAN**
DIRECTED BY
MIKE NICHOLS PRINTS BY PATHE **TECHNICOLOR**® **PANAVISION**®
AN EMBASSY PICTURES RELEASE

14

The Cincinnati Kid (1965)
British 30 × 40 in. (76 × 102 cm)

The Thomas Crown Affair (1968)
US 41 × 27 in. (104 × 69 cm)

Love With The Proper Stranger (1963)
US 41 × 27 in. (104 × 69 cm)

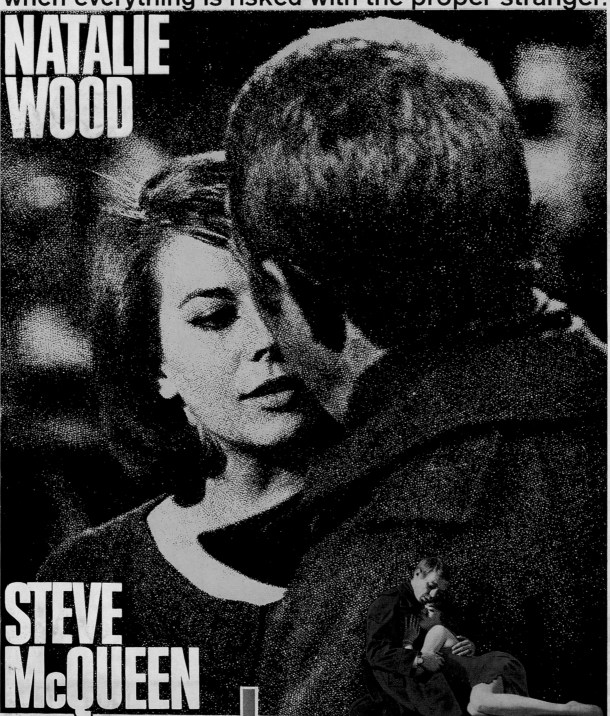

There is a moment—a long moment—
when everything is risked with the proper stranger.

NATALIE WOOD

STEVE McQUEEN

IN A PAKULA-MULLIGAN PRODUCTION

LOVE WITH THE PROPER STRANGER

WRITTEN BY ARNOLD SCHULMAN

Co-starring EDIE ADAMS

Also co-starring HERSCHEL BERNARDI and introducing TOM BOSLEY Produced by ALAN J. PAKULA · Directed by ROBERT MULLIGAN · Music—ELMER BERNSTEIN · A PARAMOUNT RELEASE

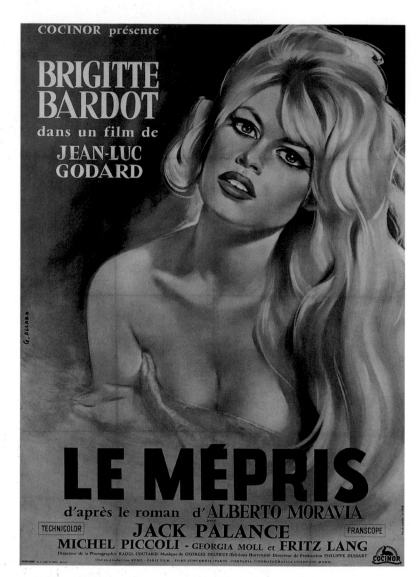

L'Amour A 20 Ans (Love At 20)
(1962)
French 63 × 47 in. (160 × 119 cm)

Le Mepris (1963)
French 63 × 47 in. (160 × 119 cm)
Art by Georges Allard

Belle De Jour (1967)
French 31 × 24 in. (79 × 61 cm)
Art by René Ferracci

**Breakfast At Tiffany's / Desayuno
Con Diamantes** (1961)
Spanish 39 × 28 in. (99 × 71 cm)
Art by Martí, Clave, Pico (MCP)

Belle De Jour (1967)
Japanese 60 × 20 in. (152 × 51 cm)

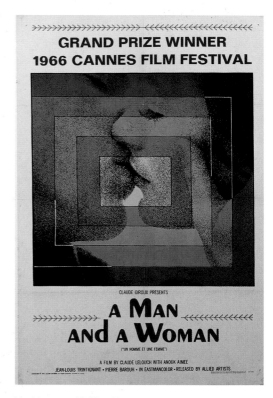

Un Homme Et Une Femme
(A Man And A Woman) (1966)
US 41 × 27 in. (104 × 69 cm)

Un Homme Et Une Femme
(A Man And A Woman) (1966)
Japanese 30 × 20 in. (76 × 51 cm)

Sweet Bird Of Youth (1962)
US 41 × 27 in. (104 × 69 cm)

The Hustler (1961)
US 41 × 27 in. (104 × 69 cm)
(Re-release 1964)

The man...and the motion picture that simply do not conform.

PAUL NEWMAN
COOL HAND LUKE

CO-STARRING GEORGE KENNEDY · J. D. CANNON ROBERT DRIVAS · LOU ANTONIO STROTHER MARTIN and JO VAN FLEET DIRECTED BY STUART ROSENBERG · PRODUCED BY GORDON CARROLL SCREENPLAY BY DONN PEARCE and FRANK R. PIERSON Music by Lalo Schifrin TECHNICOLOR® PANAVISION® FROM WARNER BROS.-SEVEN ARTS W

Copyright (c) 1967 Warner Bros.-Seven Arts Printed in U.S.A. 67/377

You never met
a pair like Butch
and The Kid

They're Taking Trains...
They're Taking Banks
And They're Taking
One Piece Of Baggage!

20th Century-Fox presents

PAUL NEWMAN
ROBERT REDFORD
KATHARINE ROSS

BUTCH CASSIDY A

A George Roy Hill–Paul Monash Production. Co-St
Executive Producer PAUL MONASH   Produced by JOHN FORE
Music Composed and Conducted by BURT BACHARACH   A NEW

Butch Cassidy And The Sundance Kid
(1969)
British 30 × 40 in. (76 × 102 cm)

D THE SUNDANCE KID 'A'

TROTHER MARTIN,   JEFF COREY,   HENRY JONES.

Directed by GEORGE ROY HILL Written by WILLIAM GOLDMAN
FOREMAN Presentation PANAVISION® COLOUR BY DE LUXE

Printed in England by Lonsdale & Bartholomew (Nottingham) Ltd.

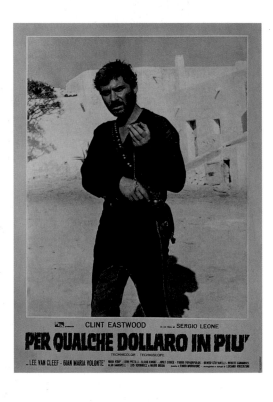

**Per Qualche Dollaro In Piu
(For A Few Dollars More)** (1966)
Italian 37 × 26 in. (94 × 66 cm)
(Set of 3)

**Per Qualche Dollaro In Piu
(For A Few Dollars More)** (1966)
Italian 79 × 55 in. (201 × 140 cm)
Art by Franco Fiorenzi

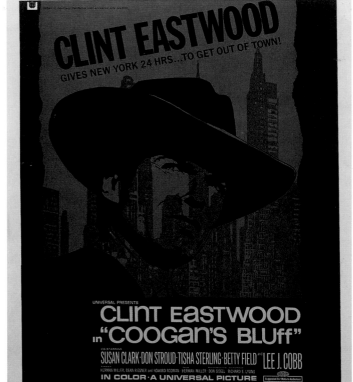

Coogan's Bluff (1968)
US 22 × 14 in. (56 × 36 cm)

Midnight Cowboy (1969)
US 41 × 27 in. (104 × 69 cm)
Photograph by Steve Schapiro

Fistful Of Dollars (1964)
US 41 × 27 in. (104 × 69 cm)
(Advance)

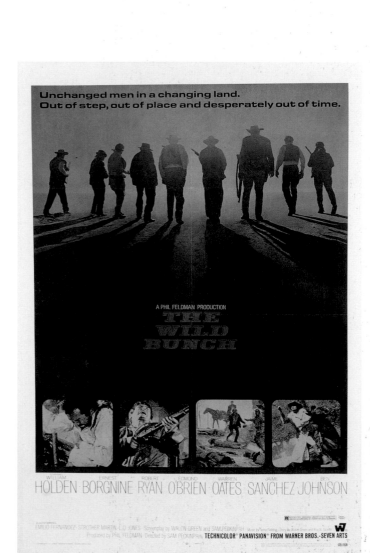

The Wild Bunch (1969)
US 41 × 27 in. (104 × 69 cm)

A JEROME HELLMAN–JOHN SCHLESINGER PRODUCTION

DUSTIN HOFFMAN
JON VOIGHT

"MIDNIGHT COWBOY"

BRENDA VACCARO   JOHN McGIVER   RUTH WHITE   SYLVIA MILES   BARNARD HUGHES

Screenplay by WALDO SALT Based on the novel by JAMES LEO HERLIHY Produced by JEROME HELLMAN Directed by JOHN SCHLESINGER·

Music Supervision by JOHN BARRY "EVERYBODY'S TALKIN'" sung by NILSSON ORIGINAL MOTION PICTURE SCORE AVAILABLE ON UNITED ARTISTS RECORDS

COLOR by DeLuxe

 PERSONS UNDER 17 NOT ADMITTED

 United Artists
Entertainment from Transamerica Corporation

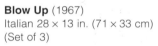

Blow Up (1967)
Italian 28 × 13 in. (71 × 33 cm)
(Set of 3)

Bob & Carol & Ted & Alice (1969)
US International 41 × 27 in. (104 × 69 cm)

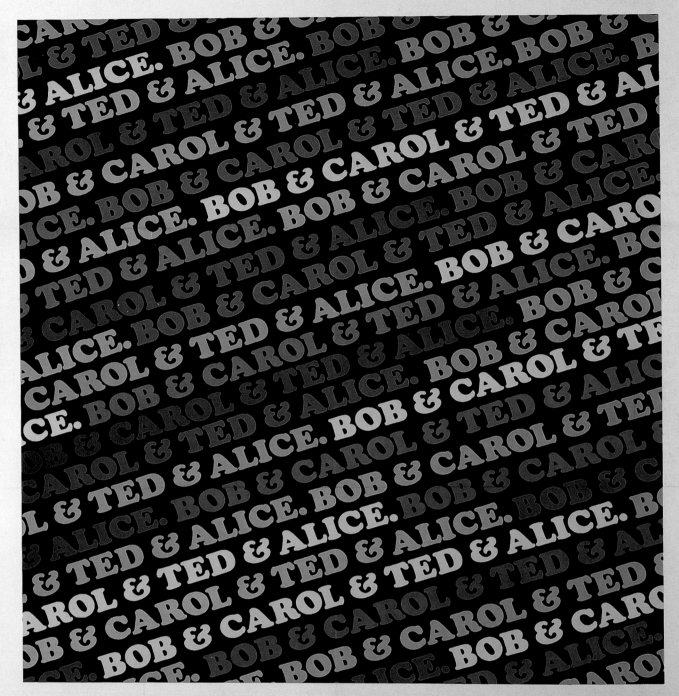

consider the possibilities

COLUMBIA PICTURES presents
A FRANKOVICH PRODUCTION

NATALIE WOOD   ROBERT CULP

BOB & CAROL & TED & ALICE

ELLIOTT GOULD   DYAN CANNON

Written by PAUL MAZURSKY and LARRY TUCKER • Music by QUINCY JONES
Executive Producer M. J. FRANKOVICH • Technicolor®
Produced by LARRY TUCKER • Directed by PAUL MAZURSKY

Soundtrack Album Available on Bell Records

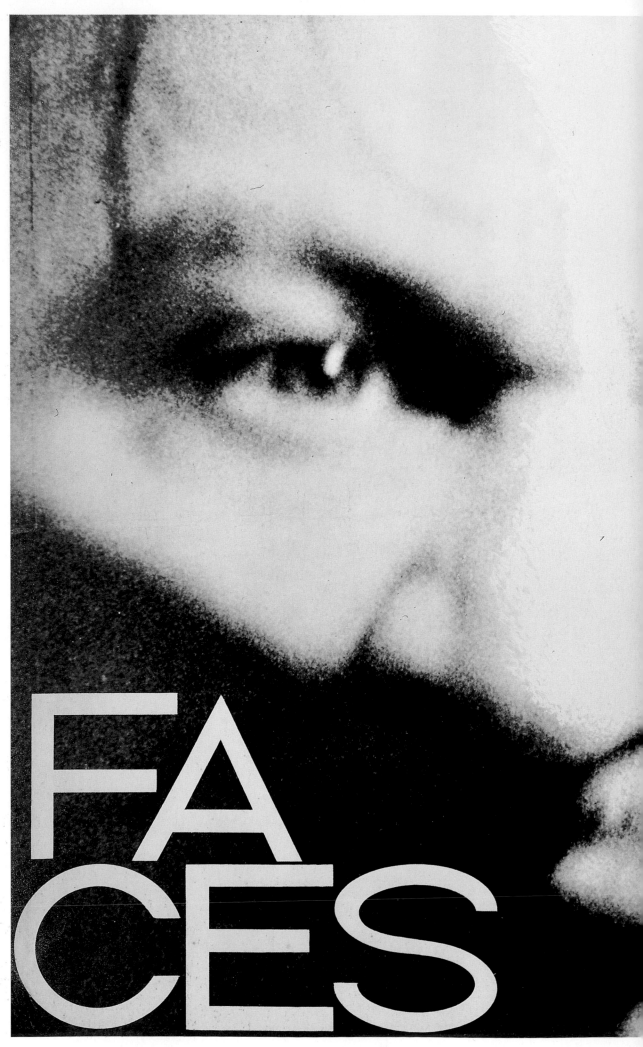

Faces (1968)
US 22 × 28 in. (56 × 71 cm)

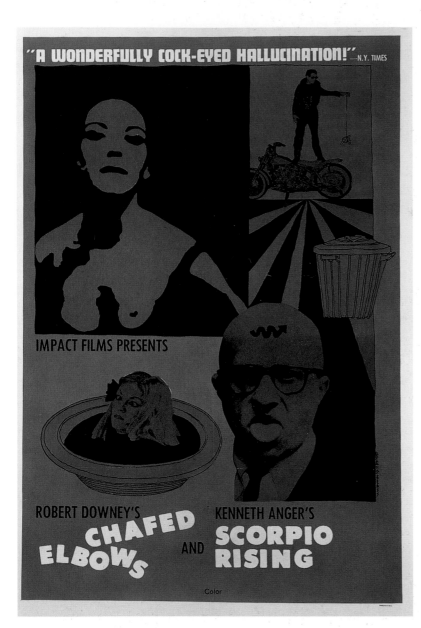

Chafed Elbows And Scorpio Rising
(1965)
US 41 × 27 in. (104 × 69 cm)
Art by David Weissmann

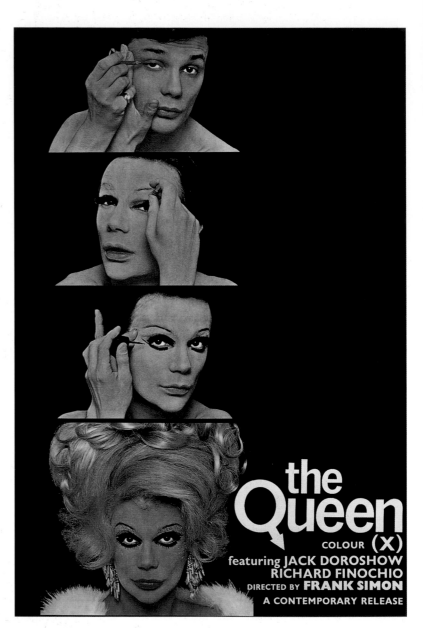

The Queen (1968)
British 30 × 20 in. (76 × 51 cm)

Film polski

nóż w wodzie

Reżyseria: Roman Polański

Produkcja: ZRF „Kamera"

Zdjęcia: Jerzy Lipman

W rolach głównych: Jolanta Umecka Leon Niemczyk Zygmunt Malanowicz

Acid - Delirio Dei Sensi (1968)
Italian 39 × 80 in. (99 × 203 cm)

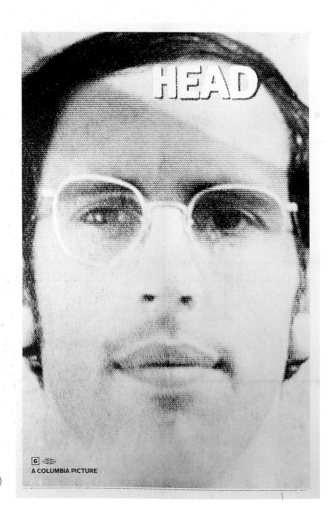

Head (1968)
US 41 × 27 in. (104 × 69 cm)
(Style C)

Prison (1965)
US 28 × 22 in. (71 × 56 cm)
(Mixed Media On Paper)
Art by Andy Warhol

Chelsea Girls (1966)
British 30 × 20 in. (76 × 51 cm)
Art by Alan Aldridge

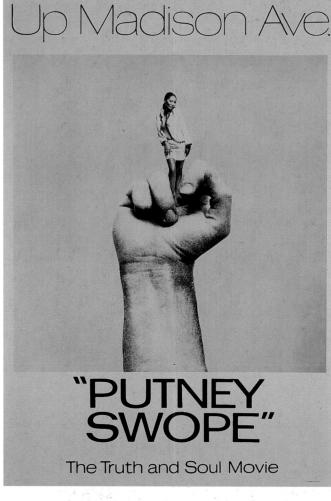

Putney Swope (1969)
US 41 × 27 in. (104 × 69 cm)

Mondo Cane / Pieski Swiat (1961)
Polish 33 × 23 in. (84 × 58 cm)
Art by Wojciech Zamecznik

The Cool World (1966)
US 41 × 27 in. (104 × 69 cm)

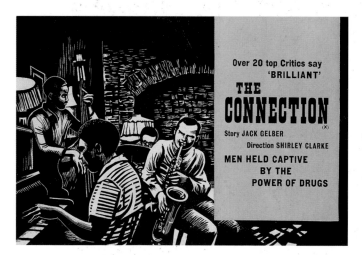

The Connection (1961)
British 30 × 40 in. (76 × 102 cm)
Art by Peter Strausfeld

Faster, Pussycat! Kill! Kill! (1966)
US 41 × 27 in. (104 × 69 cm)

Lorna (1964)
British 41 × 27 in. (104 × 69 cm)

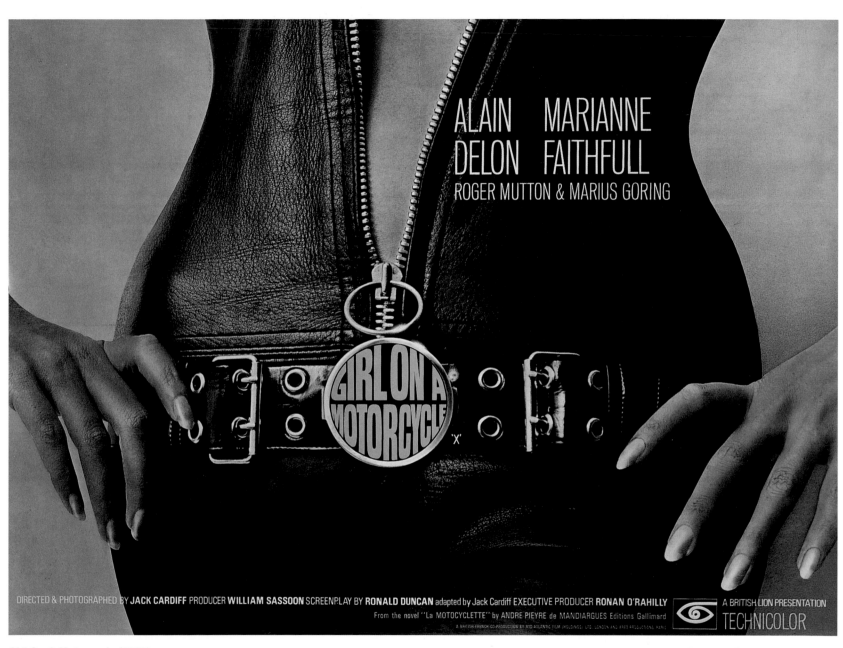

Girl On A Motorcycle (1968)
British 30 × 40 in. (76 × 102 cm)
(Style B)

"**...a hand-grenade of a film...
makes you laugh even
as your blood chills...
superb.**"
EVENING NEWS

if...

Paramount Pictures Presents
A MEMORIAL ENTERPRISES FILM   Directed by LINDSAY ANDERSON   Screenplay by DAVID SHERW
ARTHUR LOWE   PETER JEFFREY   MONA WASHBOURNE   GEOFFREY CHATER   ANTHONY NICHOLLS introducing MALCO

ced by MICHAEL MEDWIN & LINDSAY ANDERSON Colour

WELL RICHARD WARWICK CHRISTINE NOONAN DAVID WOOD ROBERT SWANN

PRINTED IN ENGLAND BY W. E. BERRY LTD., BRADFORD

If.... (1969)
British 30 × 40 in. (76 × 102 cm)

Accattone (1961)
British 30 × 40 in. (76 × 102 cm)

La Notte (1960)
Italian 13 × 38 in. (33 × 97 cm)

L' Eclisse (The Eclipse) (1962)
Italian 28 × 13 in. (71 × 33 cm)

8½ (1963)
Italian 79 × 55 in. (201 × 140 cm)

ANGELO RIZZOLI presenta

FEDERICO FELLINI

8 1/2

CON

MARCELLO MASTROIANNI
CLAUDIA CARDINALE
ANOUK AIMEE
SANDRA MILO

ROSSELLA FALK · BARBARA STEELE
GUIDO ALBERTI · MADELEINE LEBEAU
JEAN ROUGEUL · CATERINA BORATTO
E CON
ANNIBALE NINCHI · GIUDITTA RISSONE

PRODUZIONE

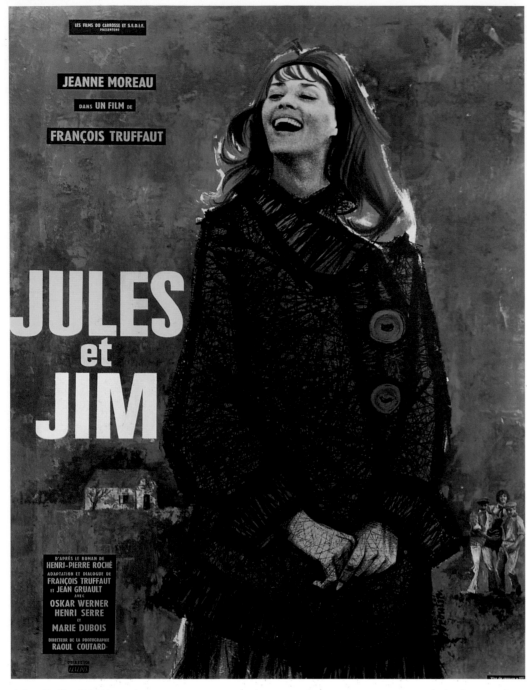

Jules Et Jim (1961)
French 63 × 47 in. (160 × 119 cm)
Art by Christian Broutin

Vivre Sa Vie (1962)
French 23 × 15 in. (58 × 38 cm)
Art by Vaissier

Pierrot Le Fou (1965)
French 63 × 47 in. (160 × 119 cm)
Art by René Ferracci

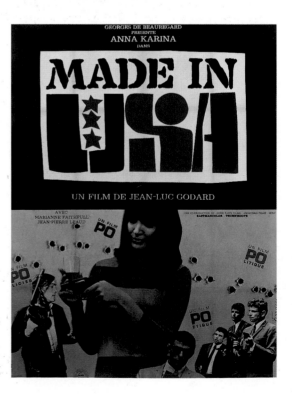

Made In USA (1966)
French 63 × 47 in. (160 × 119 cm)
Art by René Ferracci

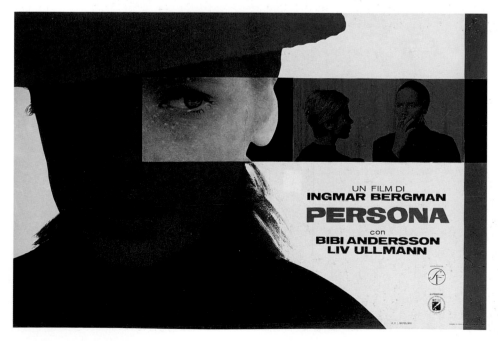

The Misfits (1961)
US 60 × 40 in. (152 × 102 cm)
(Special)
Photographs by Henri Cartier-Bresson,
Ernest Haas, Bruce Davidson, Cornell
Capa, Erich Hartman, Elliott Erwitt,
Dennis Stock, Eve Arnold, Inge Morath

Persona (1967)
Italian 19 × 27 in. (48 × 69 cm)
(Set of 3)

This Sporting Life (1963)
British 41 × 27 in. (104 × 69 cm)
Art by Renato Fratini

Saturday Night And Sunday Morning
(1960)
British 30 × 40 in. (76 × 102 cm)

The Loneliness Of The Long
Distance Runner (1962)
British 30 × 40 in. (76 × 102 cm)
Art by S. John Woods

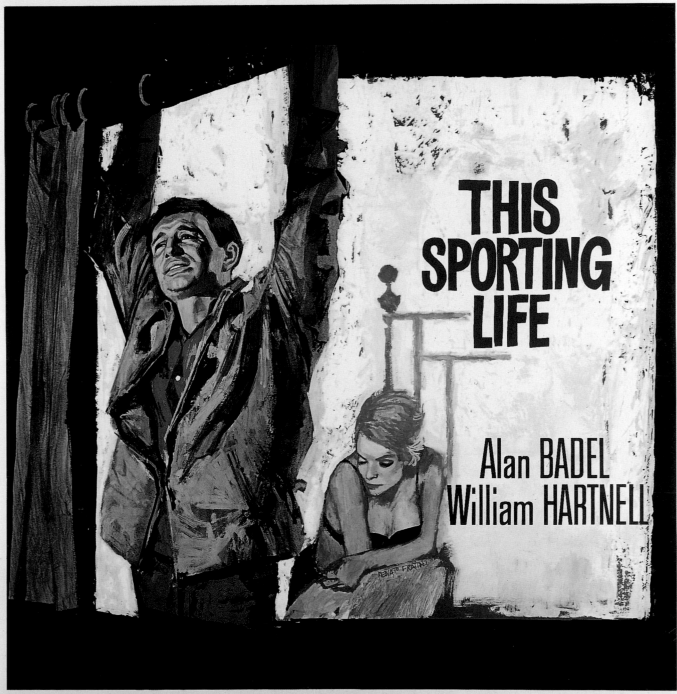

THE RANK ORGANISATION PRESENTS
A JULIAN WINTLE-LESLIE PARKYN PRODUCTION

RICHARD HARRIS
RACHEL ROBERTS

THIS SPORTING LIFE

Alan BADEL
William HARTNELL

SCREENPLAY BY DAVID STOREY
PRODUCED BY KAREL REISZ
DIRECTED BY LINDSAY ANDERSON

Printed in England.

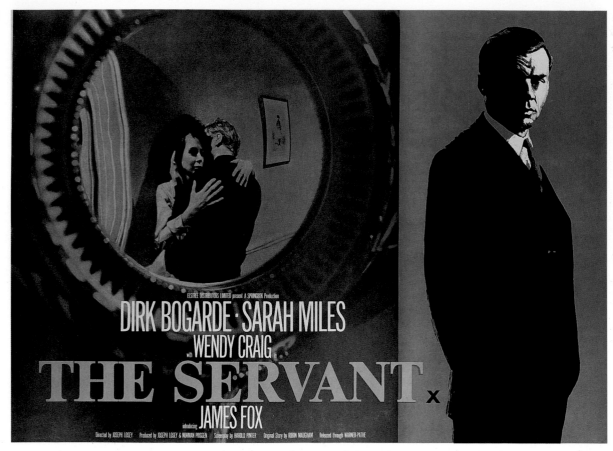

The Servant (1963)
British 30 × 40 in. (76 × 102 cm)

A Taste Of Honey (1961)
British 30 × 40 in. (76 × 102 cm)
Art by E. Apicella

The Servant (1963)
Japanese 30 × 20 in. (76 × 51 cm)

Poor Cow (1967)
German 33 × 23 in. (84 × 58 cm)
Art by Fritz Fischer

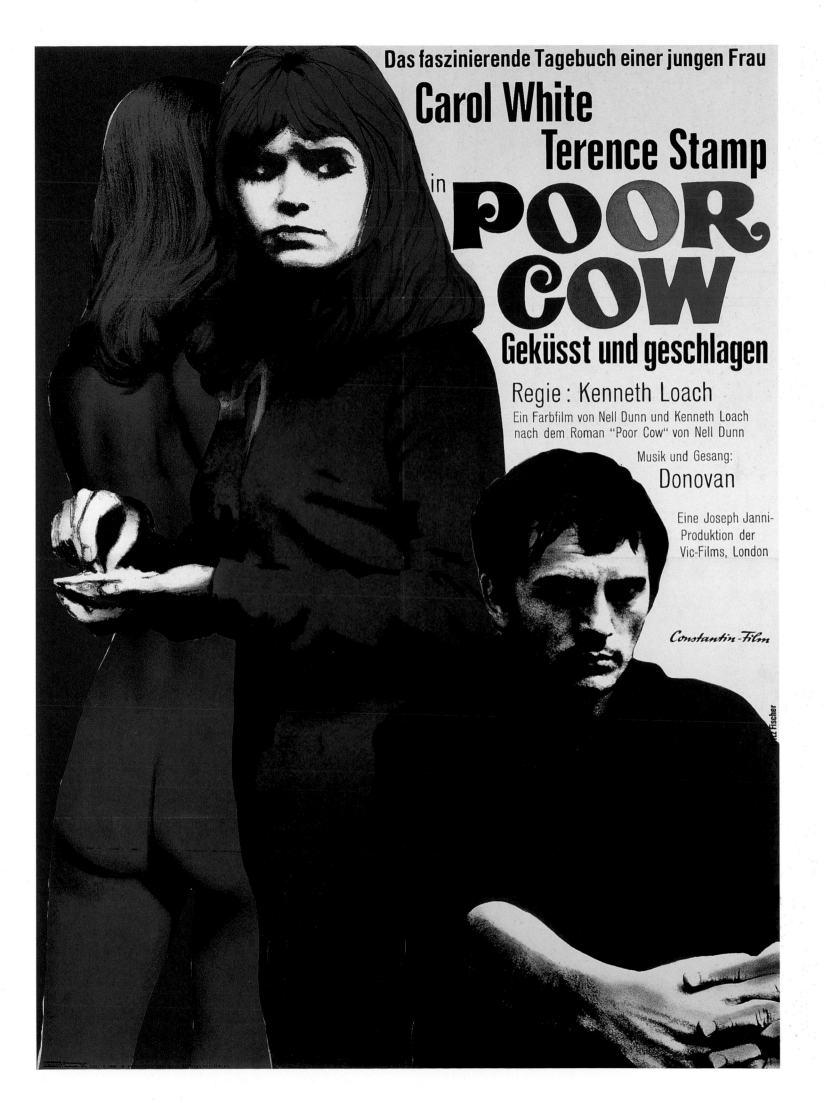

Une Femme Est Une Femme /
La Donna E Donna (1960)
Italian 27 × 18 in. (69 × 46 cm)

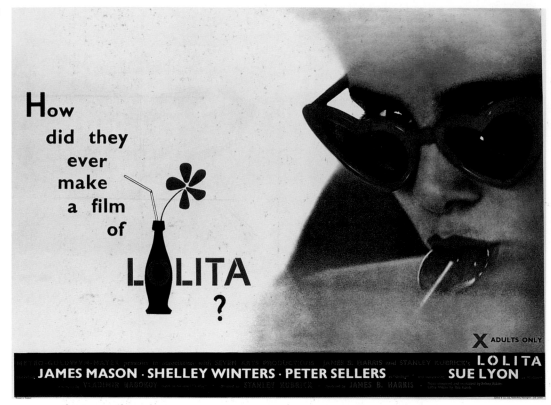

Lolita (1962)
British 30 × 40 in. (76 × 102 cm)

Darling (1965)
British 30 × 40 in. (76 × 102 cm)

JEAN-PAUL BELMONDO • JEAN-CLAUDE BRIALY e ANNA KARINA

LA DONNA È DONNA

FRANSCOPE
EASTMANCOLOR

DISTRIBUZIONE

Regia: JEAN-LUC GODARD

Soggetto, adattamento e dialoghi di JEAN-LUC GODARD • Coproduzione italo-francese: EURO INTERNATIONAL FILMS (Roma) - ROME PARIS FILMS (Parigi) • Realizzato da CARLO PONTI e GEORGES DE BEAUREGARD

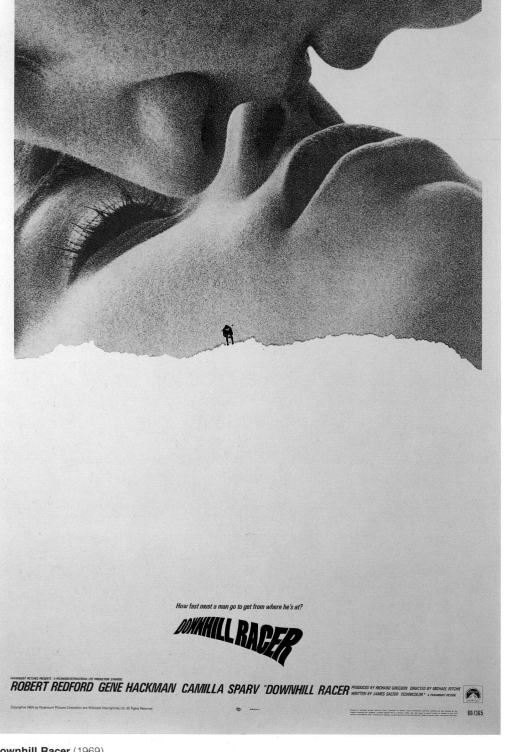

13 Jours En France /
13 Dni W Grenoble (1968)
Polish 33 × 23 in. (84 × 58 cm)

Downhill Racer (1969)
US 41 × 27 in. (104 × 69 cm)
Design by Steve Frankfurt

The Endless Summer (1966)
US 17 × 11 in. (43 × 28 cm)

The Endless Summer

On any day of the year it's summer somewhere in the world. Bruce Brown's latest color film highlights the adventures of two young American surfers, Robert August and Mike Hynson who follow this everlasting summer around the world. Their unique expedition takes them to Senegal, Ghana, Nigeria, South Africa, Australia, New Zealand, Tahiti, Hawaii and California. Share their experiences as they search the world for that perfect wave which may be forming just over the next Horizon. **BRUCE BROWN FILMS**

Bruce Brown Films the producer of "Slippery When Wet," "Surf Crazy," "Barefoot Adventure," "Surfing Hollow Days," "Waterlogged" and "The Endless Summer."

Le Testament D'Orphee (1960)
French 63 × 47 in. (160 × 119 cm)
Art by Jean Cocteau

Repulsion (1965)
British 30 × 40 in. (76 × 102 cm)
Art by Jan Lenica

Cul De Sac (1966)
British 30 × 40 in. (76 × 102 cm)
Art by Jan Lenica

Le testament d'Orphée

un film de Jean Cocteau

Une production: JEAN THUILLIER
POUR
LES ÉDITIONS
CINÉGRAPHIQUES

DISTRIBUTION
CINEDIS

Camelot (1967)
US 41 × 27 in. (104 × 69 cm)
Art by Bob Peak

The Fox (1968)
US 41 × 27 in. (104 × 69 cm)
Art by L. & D. Dillon

The Illustrated Man (1969)
British 30 × 40 in. (76 × 102 cm)

64

Rosemary's Baby (1968)
US 41 × 27 in. (104 × 69 cm)
Design by Steve Frankfurt

**La Maschera Del Demonio
(Black Sunday)** (1960)
Italian 79 × 55 in. (201 × 140 cm)
Art by Giuliano Nistri

Whatever Happened To Baby Jane?
(1962)
US 41 × 27 in. (104 × 69 cm)

Kill Baby Kill (1969)
US 41 × 27 in. (104 × 69 cm)

LA MASCHERA
DEL DEMONIO

BARBARA
STEELE · RICHARDSON · CHECCHI · GARRANI · DOMINICI
JOHN · ANDREA · IVO · ARTURO

ENRICO OLIVIERI · Regia: MARIO BAVA · PRODUZIONE: GALATEA - JOLLY FILM

Psycho (1960)
British 30 × 40 in. (76 × 102 cm)
(Style B)

Psycho / Psyco (1960)
Italian 55 × 39 in. (140 × 99 cm)

Peeping Tom (1960)
British 30 × 40 in. (76 × 102 cm)

Night Of The Living Dead (1968)
US 41 × 27 in. (104 × 69 cm)

Dracula Prince Of Darkness (1965)
British 30 × 40 in. (76 × 102 cm)

Night Of The Living Dead (1968)
British 30 × 40 in. (76 × 102 cm)

Dracula Has Risen From The Grave
(1968)
US 36 × 14 in. (91 × 36 cm)

70

Z (1969)
French 31 × 24 in. (79 × 61 cm)

Alphaville (1965)
French 63 × 47 in. (160 × 119 cm)
Art by Jean Mascii

The Manchurian Candidate (1962)
US 41 × 27 in. (104 × 69 cm)

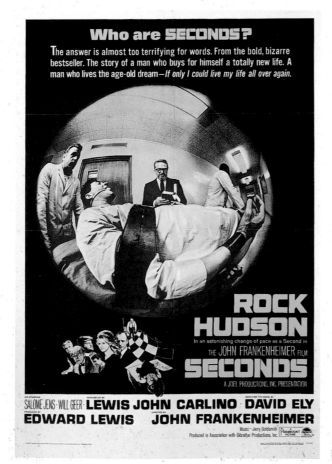

Seconds (1966)
US 41 × 27 in. (104 × 69 cm)

ANDRÉ MICHELIN présente

EDDIE CONSTANTINE

dans

ALPHAVILLE

UNE ÉTRANGE AVENTURE DE LEMMY CAUTION

UN FILM DE

JEAN-LUC GODARD

ANNA KARINA

AKIM TAMIROFF

MUSIQUE DE PAUL MISRAKI

ATHOS FILMS
DISTRIBUTION

Le Doulos (1962)
French 31 × 24 in. (79 × 61 cm)
Art by Jacques Fourastie

Le Samouraï (1967)
French 63 × 47 in. (160 × 119 cm)
Art by René Ferracci

LE SAMOURAÏ

PRODIS présente

ALAIN DELON

LE SAMOURAÏ

avec

FRANÇOIS PERIER

et

NATHALIE DELON

production
FILMEL -FILMS BORDERIE - T.C.P.
FIDA CINÉMATOGRAFICA

Producteur délégué : EUGÈNE LEPICIER

Photo de : HENRI DECAE

un film de
JEAN-PIERRE MELVILLE

Bullitt (1968)
US 41 × 27 in. (104 × 69 cm)
(Advance)

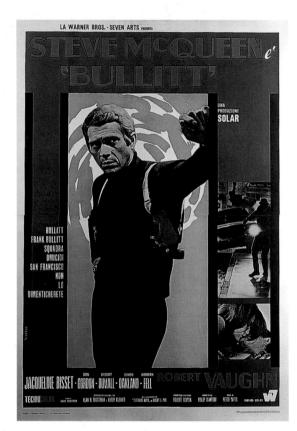

Bullitt (1968)
Italian 79 × 55 in. (201 × 140 cm)
Art by Ferrini

Bullitt (1968)
US 41 × 27 in. (104 × 69 cm)
(Style A)

Robbery (1967)
British 30 × 40 in. (76 × 102 cm)

Oceans 11 (1960)
US 36 × 14 in. (91 × 36 cm)

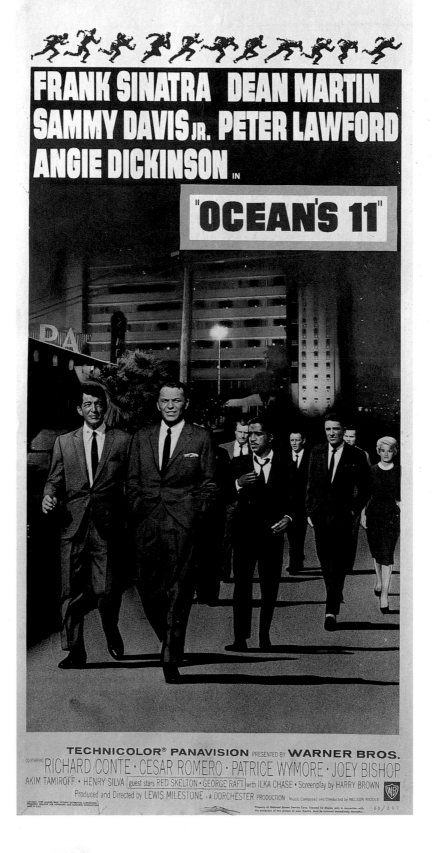

78

Bonnie And Clyde (1967)
US 41 × 27 in. (104 × 69 cm)

The Rise And Fall Of 'Legs' Diamond
(1960)
British 30 × 40 in. (76 × 102 cm)

WARREN BEATTY
FAYE DUNAWAY

They're young... they're in love

...and they kill people.

BONNIE *and* CLYDE

MICHAEL J. POLLARD · GENE HACKMAN · ESTELLE PARSONS

Written by DAVID NEWMAN and ROBERT BENTON · Music by Charles Strouse · Produced by WARREN BEATTY · Directed by ARTHUR PENN

TECHNICOLOR® FROM WARNER BROS.-SEVEN ARTS

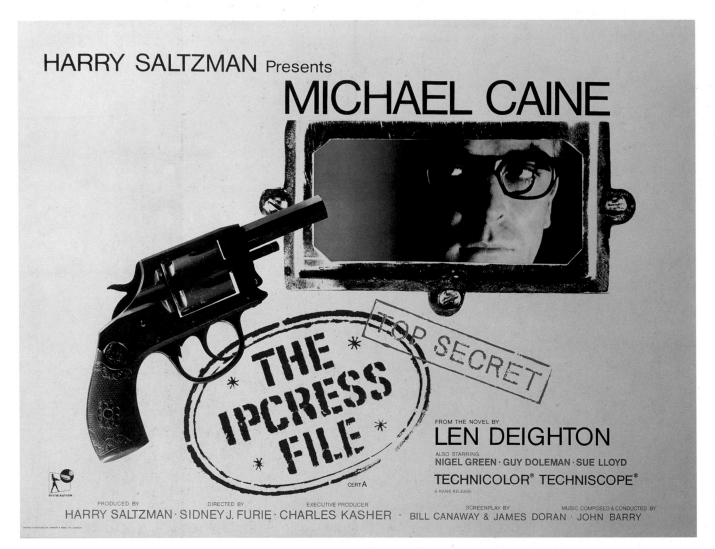

The Ipcress File (1964)
British 30 × 40 in. (76 × 102 cm)
(Style A)
Design by Eric Pullford

Point Blank / Zbieg Z Alcatraz (1967)
Polish 33 × 23 in. (84 × 58 cm)
Art by Bronislaw Zelek

Metro-Goldwyn-Mayer presents
A Judd Bernard-Irwin Winkler
Production starring

LEE MARVIN
"POINT BLANK"

**There are two kinds of people in his up-tight world:
his victims and his women. And sometimes you can't tell them apart.**

co-starring **ANGIE DICKINSON**

KEENAN WYNN · CARROLL O'CONNOR · LLOYD BOCHNER · MICHAEL STRONG

Screenplay by Alexander Jacobs and David Newhouse & Rafe Newhouse Based on the Novel "The Hunter" by Richard Stark

Directed by John Boorman. Produced by Judd Bernard and Robert Chartoff **In Panavision® and Metrocolor** MGM

Alfie (1966)
British 30 × 40 in. (76 × 102 cm)

Billion Dollar Brain (1967)
US 41 × 27 in. (104 × 69 cm)

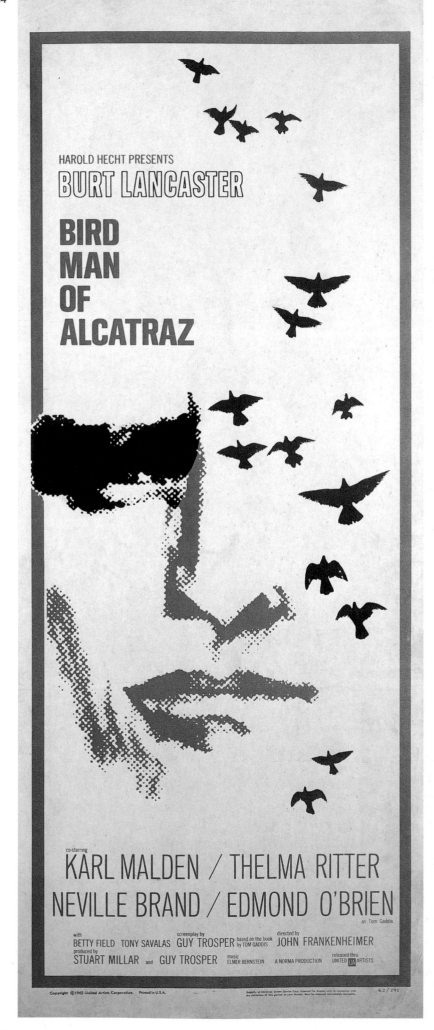

Birdman Of Alcatraz (1962)
US 36 × 14 in. (91 × 36 cm)
Art by Saul Bass

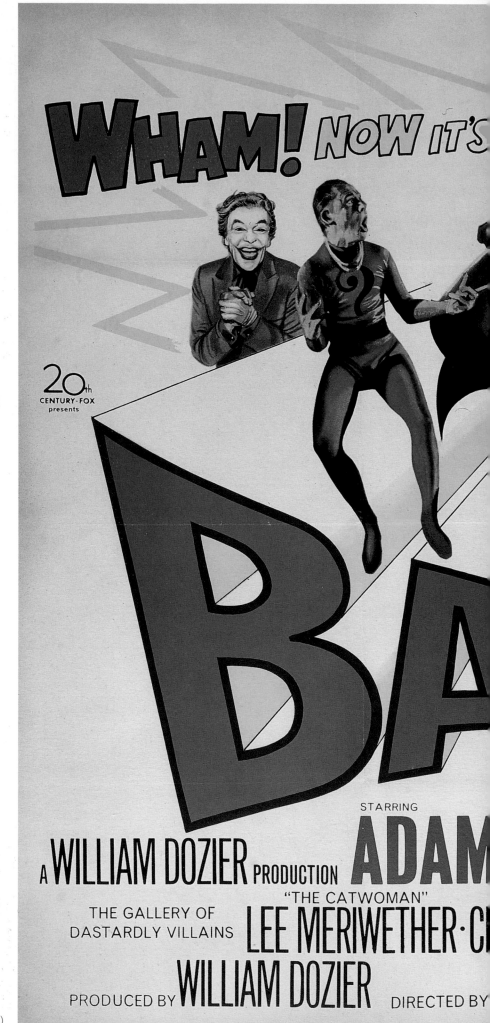

Batman (1966)
British 30 × 40 in. (76 × 102 cm)

2001: A Space Odyssey (Cinerama)
(1968)
US 41 × 27 in. (104 × 69 cm)
(Style C)
Art by Robert McCall

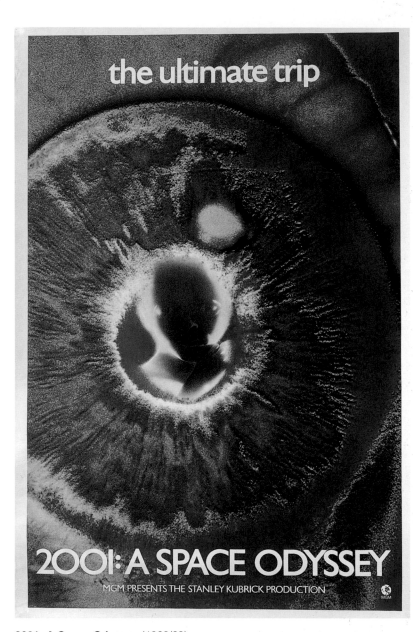

2001: A Space Odyssey (1968/69)
US 41 × 27 in. (104 × 69 cm)
(Style D)

2001: A Space Odyssey (1968/69)
US 41 × 27 in. (104 × 69 cm)
(Style E)

An epic drama of adventure and exploration

...taking you half a billion miles from Earth...
further from home than any man in history.
Destination: Jupiter.

MGM PRESENTS A STANLEY KUBRICK PRODUCTION

2001
a space odyssey

CINERAMA Super Panavision® and Metrocolor

Fantastic Voyage (1966)
US 41 × 27 in. (104 × 69 cm)

Fantastic Voyage (1966)
US 22 × 14 in. (56 × 36 cm)
(Special Advance)

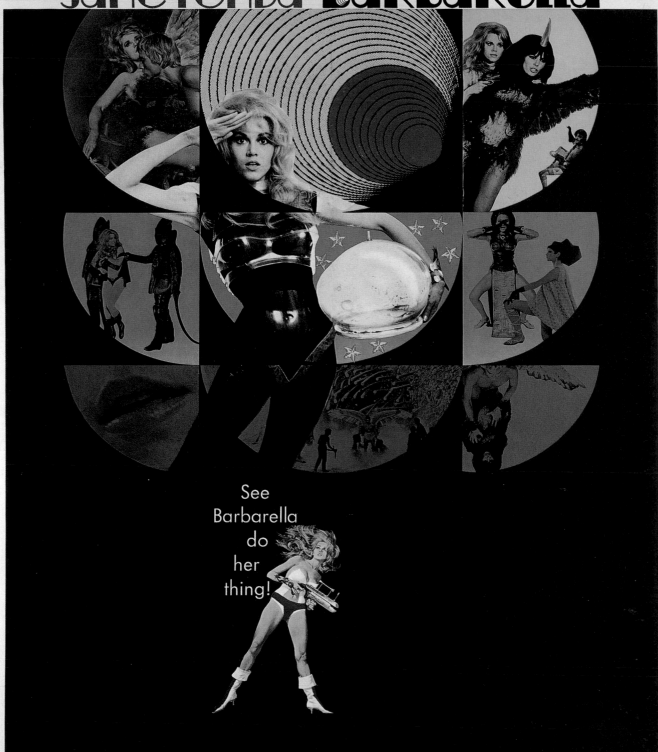

**Terrore Nello Spazio
(Planet Of The Vampires)** (1965)
Italian 28 × 13 in. (71 × 33 cm)
Art by Averardo Ciriello

The Time Machine (1960)
British 30 × 40 in. (76 × 102 cm)

Dr. Who And The Daleks (1965)
British 30 × 40 in. (76 × 102 cm)

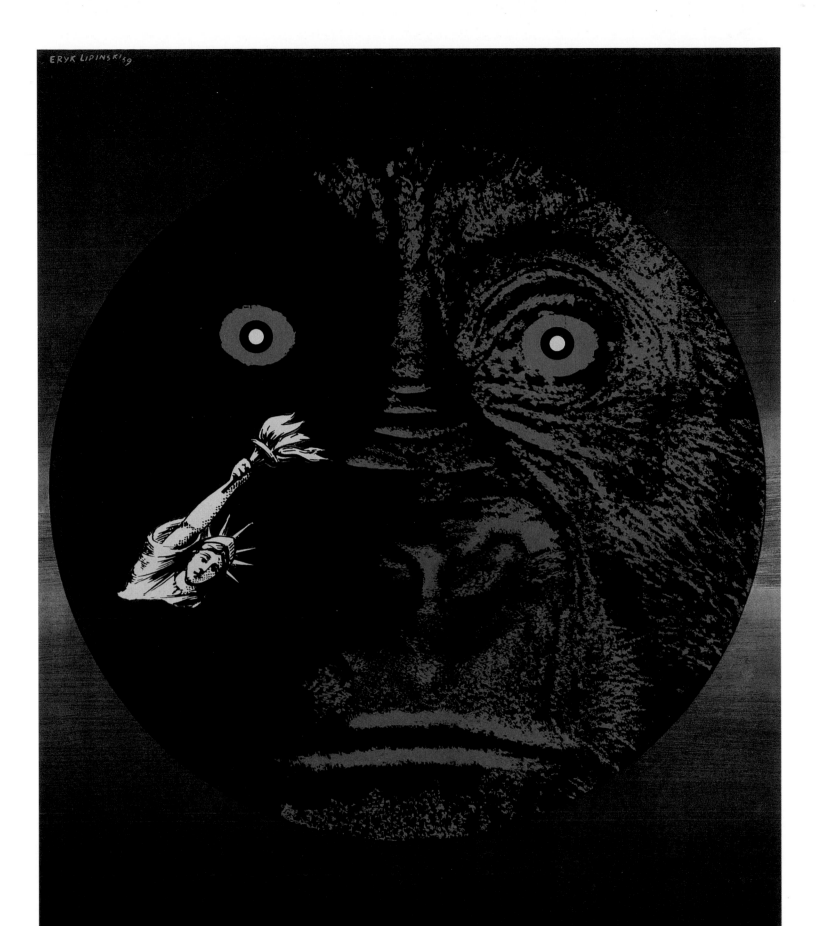

PLANETA MAŁP

96

The Longest Day (1962)
US 81 × 41 in. (206 × 104 cm)

Hell In the Pacific (1969)
British 30 × 40 in. (76 × 102 cm)

42 INTERNATIONAL STARS!

DARRYL F. ZANUCK'S

THE LONGEST DAY

FROM THE BOOK BY
CORNELIUS RYAN
RELEASED BY
20.
Century-Fox

The Great Escape (1963)
British 30 × 40 in. (76 × 102 cm)

Where Eagles Dare (1968)
US 36 × 14 in. (91 × 36 cm)

TRAIN THEM! EXCITE THEM! ARM THEM!

...THEN TURN THEM LOOSE ON THE NAZIS!

In 70 mm.
wide screen
and full
stereophonic
sound!

METRO-
GOLDWYN-
MAYER presents
A KENNETH HYMAN
PRODUCTION

The Dirty Dozen

Starring LEE **MARVIN** ERNEST **BORGNINE** CHARLES **BRONSON** JIM **BROWN** JOHN **CASSAVETES** RICHARD **JAECKEL**

GEORGE **KENNEDY** TRINI **LOPEZ** RALPH **MEEKER** ROBERT **RYAN** TELLY **SAVALAS** CLINT **WALKER** ROBERT **WEBBER**

screenplay by NUNNALLY JOHNSON and LUKAS HELLER From the novel by E.M. NATHANSON Produced by KENNETH HYMAN Directed by ROBERT ALDRICH   IN **METROCOLOR**   MGM

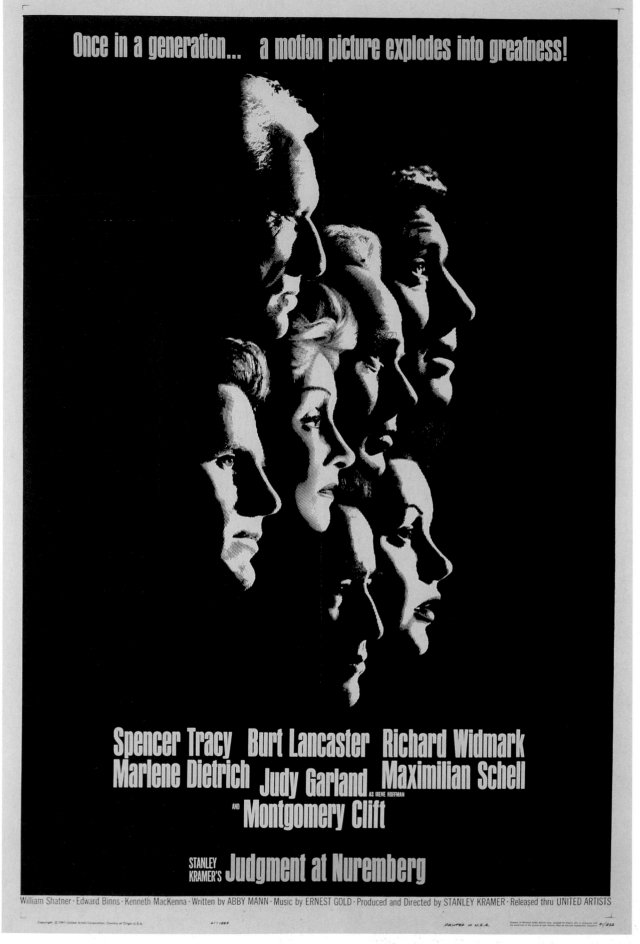

Judgement At Nuremberg (1961)
US 41 × 27 in. (104 × 69 cm)

Lawrence Of Arabia (1962)
US 41 × 27 in. (104 × 69 cm)
(Roadshow)

Cleopatra / Kleopatra (1963)
Polish 33 × 23 in. (84 × 58 cm)
Art by Eryk Lipinski

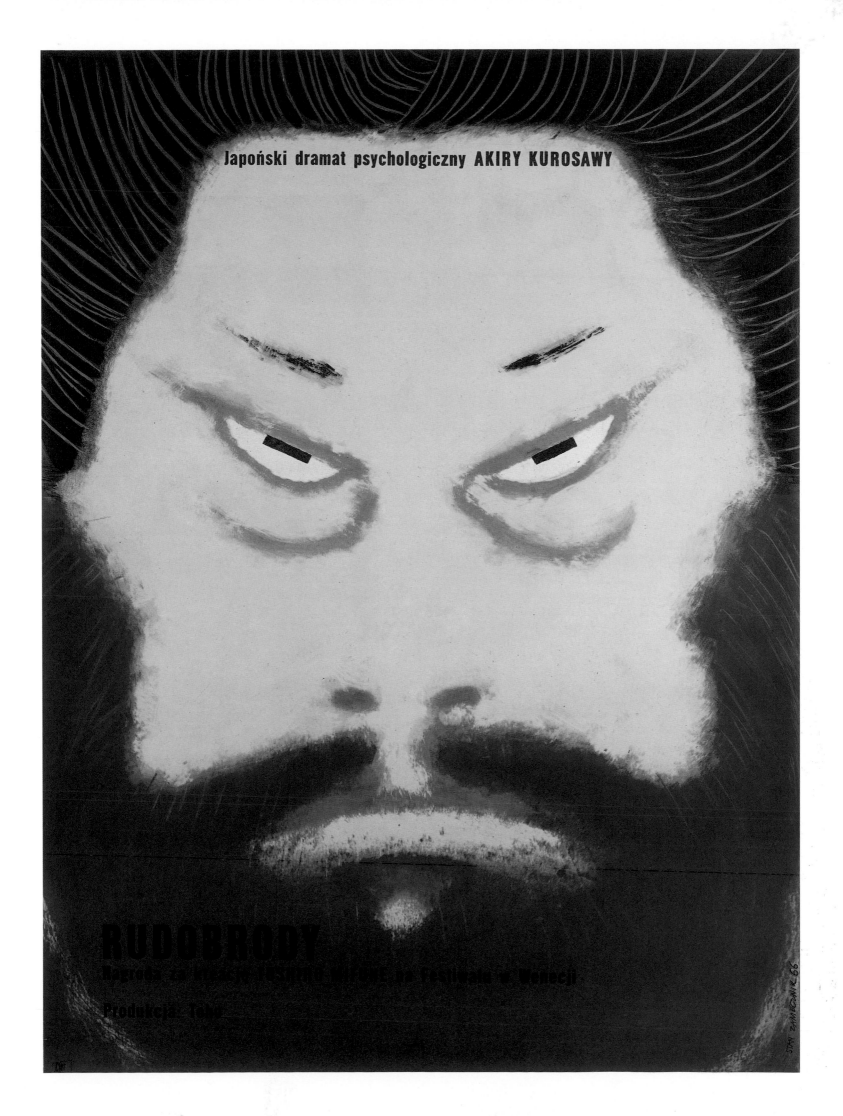

104

The Miracle Worker (1962)
US 41 × 27 in. (104 × 69 cm)

Lilith (1964)
US 22 × 28 in. (56 × 71 cm)

'the Miracle Worker'

a great motion picture starring Anne Bancroft and introducing Patty Duke

Victor Jory with Inga Swenson, Andrew Prine & Kathleen Comegys. Screenplay by William Gibson based upon his stage play.
Music composed by Laurence Rosenthal. Produced by Fred Coe. Directed by Arthur Penn. Released thru United Artists

French Dressing (1963)
British 41 × 27 in. (104 × 69 cm)

Play Time (1967)
French 31 × 24 in. (79 × 61 cm)
Art by Baudin
Design by René Ferracci

テオレマ

'68年ベネチア映画祭O.C.I.C賞／女優演技賞■シルバーナ・マンガーノ／テレンス・スタンプ主演■監督ピエル・パオロ・パゾリーニ　カラー作品

音楽エンニオ・モリコーネ／主題曲〈サントラ盤〉キング・レコード／撮影ジュゼッペ・ルッツォリーニ／イタリア映画　東和提供

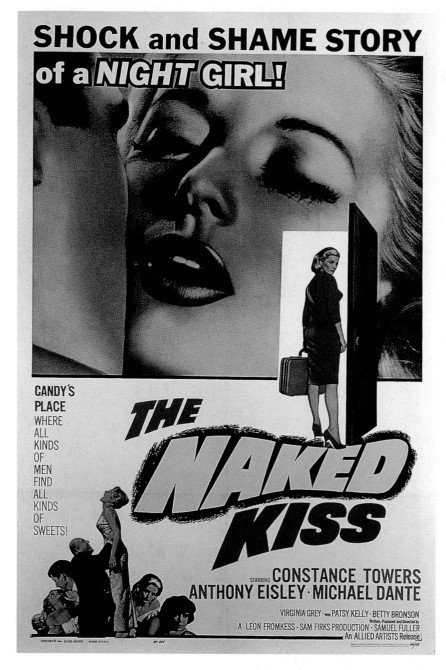

The Naked Kiss (1964)
US 41 × 27 in. (104 × 69 cm)

Irma La Douce (1963)
British 30 × 40 in. (76 × 102 cm)

Goldfinger (1964)
British 30 × 40 in. (76 × 102 cm)
(Style A)

JAMES BOND BACK IN ACTION!

ALBERT R. BROCCOLI &
HARRY SALTZMAN PRESENT

SEAN CONNERY AS
JAMES BOND 007

IN IAN FLEMING'S

GOLDFINGER Ⓐ

HONOR BLACKMAN
AS PUSSY GALORE
GERT FROBE
AS GOLDFINGER

TECHNICOLOR ®

UNITED ARTISTS

SCREEN PLAY BY RICHARD MAIBAUM & PAUL DEHN
PRODUCED BY HARRY SALTZMAN & ALBERT R. BROCCOLI
DIRECTED BY GUY HAMILTON   EON PRODUCTIONS LTD

Dr. No (1962)
British 30 × 40 in. (76 × 102 cm)

Thunderball (1965)
British 30 × 40 in. (76 × 102 cm)

From Russia With Love (1963)
British 30 × 40 in. (76 × 102 cm)
Art by Renato Fratini

You Only Live Twice (1967)
British 30 × 40 in. (76 × 102 cm)
(Style B)

Casino Royale (1967)
US 60 × 20 in. (152 × 51 cm)
(Set of 6)

Casino Royale (1967)
US 22 × 14 in. (56 × 36 cm)

Modesty Blaise (1966)
US 41 × 27 in. (104 × 69 cm)
Art by Bob Peak

In Like Flint (1967)
US 41 × 27 in. (104 × 69 cm)
Art by Bob Peak

118

The Trial / El Proceso (1962)
Spanish 39 × 28 in. (99 × 71 cm)
Art by Francisco Fernandez Zarza
(Jano)

UN CHIEN ANDALOU

UN FILM DE LUIS BUÑUEL ET SALVADOR DALI

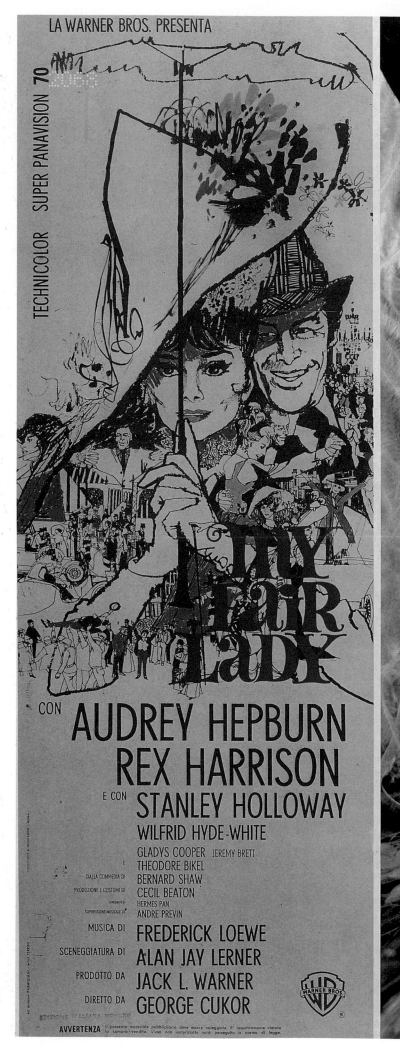

My Fair Lady (1964)
Italian 27 × 36 in. (69 × 91 cm)
(Style A)
Design by Ferrini
Photograph by Cecil Beaton

Summer Holiday (1962)
British 41 × 27 in. (104 × 69 cm)

Get Yourself A College Girl (1964)
US 41 × 27 in. (104 × 69 cm)

THE SCREEN ACHIEVES ONE OF THE GREAT ENTERTAINMENTS

IN THE HISTORY OF MOTION PICTURES

MIRISCH PICTURES PRESENTS
"WEST SIDE STORY"
A ROBERT WISE
PRODUCTION

STARRING NATALIE WOOD

RICHARD BEYMER   RUSS TAMBLYN
RITA MORENO   GEORGE CHAKIRIS
DIRECTED BY ROBERT WISE AND JEROME ROBBINS SCREENPLAY BY ERNEST LEHMAN
ASSOCIATE PRODUCER SAUL CHAPLIN / CHOREOGRAPHY BY JEROME ROBBINS
MUSIC BY LEONARD BERNSTEIN LYRICS BY STEPHEN SONDHEIM
BASED UPON THE STAGE PLAY PRODUCED BY ROBERT E. GRIFFITH and HAROLD S. PRINCE
BOOK BY ARTHUR LAURENTS
PLAY CONCEIVED, DIRECTED AND CHOREOGRAPHED BY JEROME ROBBINS
PRODUCTION DESIGNED BY BORIS LEVEN / FILMED IN PANAVISION® 70 / TECHNICOLOR®
PRESENTED BY MIRISCH PICTURES, INC. / IN ASSOCIATION WITH SEVEN ARTS PRODUCTIONS, INC.
RELEASED THRU UNITED ARTISTS

WEST
SIDE
STORY

A Hard Day's Night (1964)
British 30 × 40 in. (76 × 102 cm)
Design & Photography by Robert
Freeman

Help! (1965)
British 30 × 40 in. (76 × 102 cm)

Yellow Submarine (1968)
British 30 × 40 in. (76 × 102 cm)
Art by Heinz Edelmann

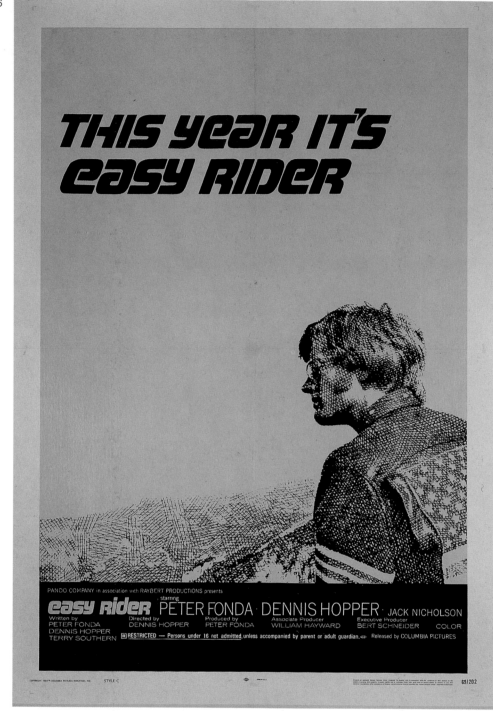

Easy Rider (1969)
US 41 × 27 in. (104 × 69 cm)

Monterey Pop (1969)
US 41 × 27 in. (104 × 69 cm)
Art by Tomi Ungerer

Easy Rider (1969)
Italian 19 × 27 in. (48 × 69 cm)

Don't Look Back (1967)
US 41 × 27 in. (104 × 69 cm)